Typhoid August
Sarah Fletcher

smith|doorstop

Published 2018 by Smith|Doorstop Books
The Poetry Business
Campo House
54 Campo Lane
Sheffield S1 2EG
www.poetrybusiness.co.uk

Copyright © Sarah Fletcher 2018
All Rights Reserved

ISBN 978-1-912196-09-8
Designed & Typeset by Utter
Printed by Biddles

Smith|Doorstop books are a member of Inpress: www.inpressbooks.co.uk. Distributed by NBN International, Airport Business Centre, 10 Thornbury Road Plymouth PL 6 7PP.

The Poetry Business gratefully acknowledges the support of Arts Council England.

Contents

5	
6	Cordelia
7	Christina Crashes The Wedding
8	The Meeting
9	For Courtney Stodden
10	Blue & Typhoid Mary (1)
11	Worthy
12	Psychology
13	
15	The Occupant
16	Hair
17	Whiskey-five
18	Blue & Typhoid Mary (2)
19	Capitulation
21	
22	Typhoid August
26	Acknowledgements

Should I believe that I have been stricken?
Does my face show some kind of glow?
– David Bowie, 'Station to Station'.

Troll me the sources of that Song
– John Berryman, 'A Professor's Song'

Have, John, you heard these days whether she's chaste?

*– She certainly has run herself into
a corner, pet.*

*And is she occupied
or subject? To or by?*

*– I saw the streetlight
prismed through their kiss. I think that says enough.
Even I could see the colours. She was necked.
The rays asserted patterns on the pavement.*

And then?

*– The two of them became their own
menagerie. From one co-regent to
the other. Seamless.*

John, indeed.

*– At least
you are no longer braided in his jacket's
silky insides.*

Not just to his, but hers as well.

*– I will say one thing, pet. Since this hatched from
your eyes, look at your face. It is the cleanest
it has been for years.*

Cordelia

In a stranger's house   she waltzes with my boyfriend
to Mahler   and tells me about emotional labour   and that I am much younger

Her name is so moneyed   I could call her Lulu or Allegra and she'd
respond   When she is tired of waltzing   she twists

her arms around Peter   who is passing out on the sofa   and says she
can tell I don't trust other women   *No darling   just you*

Her voice is a wire coat-hanger   I hang what I want on it
but now   the gin stinging my teeth   I only want her to admit

she's taken dance lessons   and who paid for them   She dresses beautifully
like the girl who bullied the school shooter   and in another life

we get cappuccinos and she tells me what sex with my boyfriend is like
focusing mainly on the lingerie she wore   and how she wouldn't let

him touch her until she could tell he was so hot   he would
come immediately when she permitted it   I've never seen a smile so white

as when she tells me how she washed the semen from his stomach in
the porcelain sink   and how many times he said sorry

Christina Crashes The Wedding

She is invited because she'd be noticed more by her absence
and her absence would be seen   by the other guests
I see her at the reception   mouthing ABBA to my husband   SOS
Her smile a conspiratorial hand-squeeze   The way she flirts   ça va?
She is calling my name   but the Ministry told me mishearings
are to be expected   from a bride of my unusually young age

I recognise the curl of her nails   from the times she's held my mouth open
to pour Malbec   through my lips   Tonight it's the good stuff
the richest pinot noir   and most of it gets on my milk-web dress
My groom says   *you should have worn a bra*   *it's winter*
The stiff tips of my nipples give the wrong signal   Somehow I enjoy this
Somehow   this is what I wanted and   uh oh sweet wife the Ministry
is sorry to report   there are Christinas everywhere
                                        you better hide the groom

The Meeting

Of course, it is also hard for him –
blood spins through his body
in unpredictable ways.
Flush digs down his neck like fruit juice
on the whitest tablecloth you can imagine.
His creaky gaze disassembles every room
he enters.

Look at him now,
sitting across from me at the wooden
table, thinking of all the places he can
injure so I can kiss it better.

For Courtney Stodden

When I see her photograph   I see a checklist of curls
kitten-tongue pink and fluff   I am consumed by seeing her
By what it means to see her   I imagine her body against
another's like fresh meat   against bad   Butchery

When she announces her pregnancy   I
imagine Baby   inside her growing   its cells like the beads of water
left after a shower
She could have a changeling   She could deliver twins
She could have two towers   with limbs as light as strings

When I was six   and she was six   I was asked to imagine
two thousand and nine hundred corpses   Just try   You can't
When I was eight I wrote a list   of things I'd say to
Osama Bin Laden

I imagine the pornography   they found in the compound
I think the girl would feel at home in it

It is my guilt that will do me in   It is the thought of her body
the thought of Baby   the thought of towers and then the counting
of bodies so I can understand   what nearly three thousand means
This starts at the chest's zero   and expands outward
It is black   It is unforgiving   It is total

Blue & Typhoid Mary (1)

Blue's chin goes slack at last call *You are always hurting me*
He goes to war with his velvet pockets to find the change   He asks
Where is my Typhoid Mary this time of night?   Does she sleep?
I say She is rinsing the hair of their children   Stealing their rings
Caring for the hairfall child by boiling dog bones for soup in the iron skillet
(the child will die in two months time regardless and at no one's expense)
I can tell he loves Mary with a love that's no one's fault   though he buys me
gin and crawls around the word divorce   like flies on mildewed bread
His smile billows like the white sail of a ship when I say I've heard
she misses him from time to time   In this air things start to matter
less   like Blue   touching his wife's back in three month's time
Like the phone ringing to tell me the news   He is touching his wife's
back   Like when in three months time   he walks me home with a delicateness
that is really tentativeness   On the pavement of Vauxhall we'll see
a dead fox's fur drink the oil of a crash   The gulls will tattle and I will know
They are telling of his hand on Mary's back   but these are things
that no longer matter   Not this air   Blue asks if I am here   I say
I feel a woman knocking with invalid love It's time to let her out

Worthy
after James Brookes

Content in rendering the carving,
what paradise will he try to mine as he lifts

the lid of unhappy cotton? He is jockey
of the slow heart, riding anger down the gangway

though it is saddled with a kiss. I learn it is not
what you want or even what you do but what

you ask for: the vessel of a dark wave breaking
into shivers, a regime of pain cocooning

into your person. Me and him,
the trappings of mercy.

The sun lurks, unwelcome, to announce
it's time to go, dragged across the sky

by a fish hook. Kiddo, these are things
we have to learn to live with.

Psychology

When his mouth unfolds   across the quiet of my back
and gives me chills   no amount of love can quell
my fear of what men's minds   wheel out when
a seventeen year old girl walks by   In these moments
no kiss can give me comfort   or reassurance
that men aren't looking past me   but rather through me
towards an imaginary sixteen year old girl   legs splayed
and smooth as wild eels   so tiny she could disappear

– Where is your woman, pet?

*Under new management.
Under things in general, like the weather
or anaesthetic. By God that girl rebelled
against her ornament.*

– What happened, pet?

*There was unearthed a steel revolver from
the grey gravel inside of her*

*– And who
unearthed it?*

All of us.

– And whose fault, pet?

*I had another lovling, whose name
became the palette of my fear and painted
the collective fantasy of man and wife
in laughable wine reds. She whimmed and wet
with every word I made, and then, each sound,
until I didn't have to speak.*

– What next?

*My woman found the lovling and she left.
Now she and her new management are swanning
across the pavement. As we speak I am breathing
the same sponge-like air that spits them in
and spins them out again.*

– And what of their condition?

I believe the term is complex, John.

The Occupant

He stayed in our flat for three months.
His body was a terrible anchor and the lichen
he brought with him soiled our couch:
the grey polyester wet, barnacled, and barely liveable.
His voice was a museum of aristocracy,
the tiny violin of his breathing shrilling us awake at night.

Still, we went on as normal.
We cooked him dinner, and ignored the tobacco
molting from his skin. Ignored the indents
on the couch when he moved, so deep
we could store bottles in their scope. We learned to love him.
First, as a pet, and then, as a landscape
in which our lives unfolded indelicately as
origami swans undressing into their paper square.

One day, he got up and left. Something about a girl.
Something blonde. Something pint in North London.
My husband and I orbited silently around each other for a week,
fixing a third drink each night in case he returned, still.
On the seventh night, my husband pulled a whiskey bottle
from the trench of a cushion. Then, two glasses. Ice. Soda.
We really have to do something about the couch, he said,
and I nodded. But we did not move, and it did not fix.

Hair

Always, I am imagining the white seam,
where hair is fastened to the scalp.
Or else, a ponytail like roped water:
the tap turning back until it's less and less,
trickling into nothing over the carpet.

The parting, eroding into God's won valley,
whether anxiousness, habit or manifest destiny,
is tugged by a hand, my own.

Whiskey-five

Five in, the three of us, sheets
to the wind, braiding together with the ease
of wave folding into wave.
Knot-hair knot-hands knot-lips but not
the formalities of love, and not the kiss
but the kiss's possibility hovering across
the pink bits of our faces as we speak.
The ease of this makes our poppy-soft heads
tilt. Language wilts to make sense of it. It brings back
no news of our wedding: three on a match
in Heaven. One, making his confession.
Two, happy as the hireling. And me,
all my hair come undone, smiling.

Blue & Typhoid Mary (2)

Typhoid Mary is kind, actually. She invites me over to her flat
so we can sort this out like adults. After the fact, she cooks
me all sorts of breakfast. I make a joke that she loves
varieties. I say that I am very happy that the two of them
could reach reconciliation. I eat only cooked things
and leave the ice cream to melt because
we all know what the State of New York did to her,
how visitors were advised to not accept even water
from her hands. Meanwhile, Blue will drink the bathwater
she dunks her feet in. He is unimpressed when I say
I want to taste through his mouth. He doesn't even know
that he is sick. Typhoid Mary is apologetic. She says
things get caught in the crossfire. The fox and me got caught
in the crossfire. Will I accept her breakfasts as a consolation?
Will that make this easier for me? I cannot stand
to hear him say he would rather be
any other colour. He is himself
and that is difficult.

Capitulation

    i.

Feigning the playfulness
of Mother-May-I   he asks
for a days-of-the-cane
throwback   I refuse

Back then I tendered my touch
more dearly   I lived in his kiss
for so long I was born in it

Now   anechoic   and him
a guerrillista of nettles and wit

I can give him what he came for
and what he now resists

    ii.

The decapitated photograph
of a torso   Sexless
in the high contrast   tender
in the anonymous lust-trade
is constant as static to my mind
like my friend describing the sting
her boyfriend draws from of her
heels tied and

does she feel like a present
as he tightens the ribbons

so tell me   what is your
luxury and who delivers it

   iii.

All the milkmaids   inconsequential
as achoo   have jostled into
wakefulness at his arrival

they are burning their hems

legs rising like the vim
of popped champagne

he says Thank You
but I did not mean to revive him

you fucking dirty pigeon of a man

*There's one thing, John, that I always return to:
my witness and their love's prehistory.
No surveillance could have apprehended how
it took only a mouth in our darkness
to bring the tabloid virus to the house.
I spotted them in Winston's, dressing themselves
in licit immortelles, as if their love had sentience itself.
My mistled eyes are trammelled by these trespasses,
and I live in the house that was once ours.
Do you know what this means?*

– Keep clear of yanks, scimitars and whiskey, pet.

Typhoid August

I first noticed things had changed
when my mother came to embrace me
and recoiled at my foreign smell

it was not me   with Typhoid
but Something Else with Typhoid

and then I began to wonder

※

I am so trans / dis-
figured   /   fixed
it is as if   I have been born
from Mary   as daughter / doubter

stricken not with Typhoid
         but with Mary

and then not stricken
but un / becoming

※

Second symptom: infection
         Its weeping wound
I am Glitch-Mouthed Girlfriend in the dirt
Lips exiled from speech   from kiss

then quarantined from kiss
thus quarantined from speech

I had to relearn how to wash my clothes
relearn how to ask for help

✳

Word left my mouth in odd shapes

I became odd shape

Not duplication of myself but new
carbon entire   and the odd wish
of wanting to un / dis exist without
converging unto death

Typhoid Mary's belief in me
willing me

What I am seeking is a corruption

✳

When she blinks I am not there
and so I long for her to sleep

✳

What I am seeking is totality
of un / dis belief   of birthmother
and Typhoid Mary This is the cure

And Yes This is a sort of begging

✳

Life in quarantine:

A vivisection of a squirrel –
its insides a neat rectangle
crushed ruby velvet

The pleasure it gives me to think
of London's ugliest, oldest alcoholic of
making love to your wife

Cigarette poised in Blue's lips
in the grooms suit anticipating
the leather-jacket photograph

Headlines, late January, 2016:
Unrest in Yemen etc. David Bowie
dead on your anniversary

I made him promise that
in the rare event of my death
he will cut off his hands
but he'd already lost
his ring finger by his own doing

*Youfuckingspoiledbrat
    dontfuckingtouchmethisflat
ismuchmoreminethanitisyours
youarefine[cryingnoise][imitation
    ofacryingnoise]*

✻

Blue and I make the same shapes
with our mouths but perhaps

· they are also built from different carbon

This makes these shapes useless
to the other

At first we thought it was fish / bicycle

How inadequate to think
fish / bicycle

It is
grief
/
Grief

Acknowledgements

Many thanks go to the editors of the following publications, in which some of these poems first appeared: *Poetry London*, *The North*, *The Scores* and *Introduction X*.

I'd like to thank Steve Dearden and The Writing Squad for giving me mentoring, support, and opportunities, as well as Lavinia Greenlaw, Jo Shapcott and the rest of my class at Royal Holloway, University of London, for reading and critiquing many of these poems in earlier versions.

I am especially in debt to those who looked at these poems during their draft stages, particularly Sam Quill, whose keen editorial input and encouragement alike helped propel the pamphlet towards completion. Other thanks must go to Imogen, Alex and Camille for their insights.

Eleanor and Suzannah, as well as the rest of The Poetry Business team, deserve a sincere thank you for their patience and effort in bringing *Typhoid August* into the world. Without them, this pamphlet would not have been possible.

Of course, the final thanks go to my mother and my father. I am eternally grateful to have a family that is loving and supportive of poetry, both that of myself and others.